Journey through

EAST FRISIA

Photos by
Günter Franz

Text by
Ulf Buschmann

Stürtz

First page:
The coast wouldn't be the coast without seagulls – as much a part of East

Frisia as any other seaside region. The screech of gulls is music to anyone who loves the sea ...

Previous page:
From Georgshöhe there are wonderful views out across the island of Norderney.

Below:
Making a ship in a bottle was once the sailor's classic pastime – and all part of the romantic image of life at sea. This traditio is today continued at the museum in Neuharlingersiel.

8

Page 10/11:
The Grosses Meer near
Aurich is a natural fen lake
and at 460 hectares or ca.

1,140 acres East Frisia's
largest inland water.
The north part is a lido,
with the southern section

a nature protection area.
The Grosses Meer is just
half to one metre deep
(ca. 1½ to 3 feet).

Contents

East Frisia: the charm of the inclement north

There is much that is unique about East Frisia; one example is Haus Schiffahrt on the island of Norderney. It was built in 1896 by the Prussian Royal Railway Company and is to this very day the only train station in Germany without any track. Haus Schiffahrt was made the headquarters of the Frisia shipping company in 1984; here, you can also buy tickets and make reservations for the German railways.

In the 1990s, when Germany's most famous East Frisian Otto Waalkes rewrote the words to Sting's equally famous hit *An Englishman in New York*, singing "Ich bin ein Friesenjung' / Und ich wohne hinterm Deich" ("I'm Frisian boy / And I live behind a dyke"), it was an ode to his homeland in the extreme northwest of Germany: East Frisia. This is a part of the country with its very own charm, unique to Europe: harsh, inclement, marked by its constant battle with the sea and the elements – yet also extremely beautiful.

The trademarks of East Frisia are lush green meadows, contentedly grazing cows, brilliant fields of rape, parks and gardens in glorious bloom or roughed up by the wind and rain, expanses of moor to which the fen settlements belong – and much more. And when a strip of land such as this is so close to the water, it's water that dominates the landscape. Ditches and canals once dug to drain the land partition the countryside like lines drawn with a ruler. Bascule bridges, dykes and the inevitable sheep that graze them and make them sturdy enough to resist the stormy sea complete the idyllic picture.

No description of East Frisia would be complete without mentioning the long sandy beaches on the seven East Frisian Islands of Borkum, Norderney, Juist, Baltrum, Langeoog, Spiekeroog and Wangerooge, the Wattenmeer or Wadden Sea, the like of which is found nowhere else in the world, and the never-ending number of stone witness to a culture going back over 2,000 years. Castles, palaces and Gulf farmhouses, lighthouses and mills have often been lovingly restored. All of these edifices can of course be visited.

The fact that the East Frisians have always been a particularly religious race is manifested in the region's countless churches. As this bit of Germany lies below sea level, these places of worship were built on man-made mounds or *Warften*. Churches built of brick are typical and

frequently found in Jeverland. They began to emerge in the 12th century and were fabricated from massive granite found in the south of Scandinavia. This building material was laboriously shipped along the many ditches and tiny canals to East Frisia – an undertaking that at that time was extremely dangerous.

Modern generations can now enjoy this cultural heritage. The churches are not just beautiful as sacred buildings in themselves; their interiors are often equally magnificent. The riches of East Frisia include over 150 historic church organs, for example, making the extreme northwest of Germany one of the most prolific organ regions in the world.

The region, its people and its language

Well into the 19th century the East Frisians had to constantly defend themselves against the unrelenting forces of nature. This has shaped their character to this very day. They only really came into any contact with the outside world – and extremely hesitantly at that – with the onset of the industrial revolution.

The East Frisians are very economical with their words. In place of a long-winded "Guten Morgen" or "Good morning", down the generations a much more succinct "Moin, moin" ("Morning") has been adopted as a universal greeting. Once you've mastered this, you will probably find that beneath the rough exterior there's a person with a big heart – friendly, but one who doesn't believe in mincing their words. East Frisians say what they think. Full stop. Once you've got to know them, you'll soon come to like them – and not just for their frankness and lack of unnecessary frills. They are reliable and stick together through thick and thin. They are loyal to the last, whether to their own family or the local community at large.

This has been expressed for centuries in the local lingo. Isolated from the other Germanic cultures, the Frisian dialect was free to develop its own quirks and idiosyncrasies. Now, however, it's completely extinct – except for on one tiny island in the Saterland southwest of Bremen. Around 2,000 people are estimated to still speak Saterland Frisian. At least *Plattdeutsch* or Low German has been upheld in the villages of East Frisia. The region between Oldenburg, the North Sea and the border to the Netherlands is considered to be the only one where *Plattdeutsch* is the usual manner of colloquial speech. East Frisia's remote location has also meant that it has kept many of its Germanic names to this very day. First names such as Zwaantje, Tjard, Thees, Ippe, Feemke, Theda, Jürn, Onno and Ocko are now gone from the rest of Germany.

Living on and with the sea

Over the centuries the East Frisians have learned to live with the sea. They know that they can't beat the wiles of nature; they have to accept them and try to exist alongside them. Those who don't lose. Living with and battling against water has caused the East Frisians to see it somewhat differently from someone in Berlin, for example. When they say "Meer" (sea) here, they mean an inland lake. The sea itself is called by its proper name: the Nordsee or North Sea. Living on and with the sea and fighting it for valuable living space has cost many lives in the past hundreds of years. Entire villages have disappeared from the face of the earth; the coastline is constantly shifting. In East Frisia's early days people settled on man-made mounds, built up above the waves. In c. 1000 the first dykes were erected. These constructions were often washed away by storm tides, however, dragging people and animals with them into oblivion.

The elemental battles fought here were logged in the monastery annals of Norden by Brother Gerrit. "In the year 1362 such a wild storm arose at around midnight on St Marcellus [January 16] that the solid buildings, churches and towers fell down and the greatest and widest trees were torn from the earth and dashed to the ground. So strong was the force of the sea that swept across the land that the Westermarsch and a large part of East Frisia were flooded. On October 9, 1373, the sea rose so high that nobody at that time could remember ever having seen a greater flood. The dykes burst."

People only started reclaiming land at the beginning of the 16th century. Hundreds of windmills were built and a system of ditches dug, retrieving valuable marshland from the sea. This is high in salt, making it extremely fertile and ideal for farming.

A long history

The history of East Frisia goes back 2,000 years, with the oldest secured documents from the late Middle Ages. Historians speak of the Freedom of Frisia, the roots of which can be traced back to c. 800. At around this time the Vikings first attacked Frisia which was then still ruled by the

Carolingians. The members of this tribe were thus exempt from military service in foreign territory. While the rest of Europe was in the firm grip of feudalism, in Frisia rule was more or less democratic, with the locals under the leadership of chieftains they elected themselves defending their Frisian privilege of freedom against any who dared to challenge it. The Emperor Charlemagne is said to have bestowed this right upon the Frisians. It stated that the Frisians did not have to tolerate rule by any lord other than the emperor of the Kingdom of Germany in the Holy Roman Empire. Legend has it that *Liber Friso* or free Frisians and their allies once conquered the Romans in Italy and were duly rewarded with their freedom. More recent research assumes that Frisia was made free by Charles the Fat in 885 following a victory over the Normans.

The empire of Free Frisia was at its pinnacle in c. 1300. It comprised 27 provinces or lands stretching from the northwest of the Netherlands through East Frisia and the Wurster Land to the north of Bremerhaven. The various communities joined forces to create the Seven Sealands, electing envoys who met each Whitsun at the legal gathering of Upstalsboom. This is on a hill in Rahe near Aurich. Two representatives from each land acted as judges; historians assume that they were from influential families, as active and passive votes were based on the amount of land a person owned. Negotiations were often extremely lengthy, especially if politics was involved. The contracts eventually agreed upon were written down in the nearby monastery of Ihlow. Politics, like the rest of life in a community, called for a system of collaboration. Defending Frisia from its enemies, including the sea, demanded that everybody help; even the young, the old and the sick were not excluded. Differences in class and rank became negligible as soon as the Frisians entered into battle with the North Sea. Everybody had the same rights – and also the same obligations. There was even a dyke law which claimed that those who did not wish to enclose their land with a sea defence would have to face the consequences.

Up until the 14th century the Frisian Empire was largely successful but then it began to crumble. The outbreak of the plague and catastrophic storm tides accelerated the process. A few influential families saw their chance and set up a system of fealty, with *hovedlinge* or headmen seizing control over certain territories. These systems were reminiscent of the older Germanic cultures in the north; the locals were obliged to serve their ruler yet were still free. The Freedom of Frisia ended in 1498 when Em-

The future has begun in East Frisia. All along the coast wind farms producing clean, renewable energy are springing up. They have been part of the landscape for many years now, such as here on the Wybelsum Polder near Emden. The sheep seem to be totally unimpressed by the giant windmills.

peror Maximilian I borrowed 300,000 guilders from Duke Albrecht of Saxony who received Frisia and Dithmarschen in return. For Frisia, a period of political division and dependence had dawned.

East Frisian sport

Where the rest of the world has football, East Frisia has *Klootschiessen*. In the northwest of Germany it's a national sport. *Klootschiessen* is similar to the German version of Irish road bowling or French *boules* played in North Germany called *Bosseln*. The object of the exercise is to throw a ball as far as you can along a fixed distance. The 'pitch' can be a field, meadow or public road. East Frisian *Klootschiessen* is much older than North German *Bosseln* and the ball-throwing technique involved quite difficult. Speed, strength and concentration are called for. In the winter months, *Klootschiessen* is something of a social event in many villages. The participants once played for items of value or money, downing one shot of spirits after another as they threw. It goes without saying that the ball often landed where it shouldn't have done and that the game frequently ended in blood flowing – first caused by the flying ball and then by fists flying in the ensuing free-for-all.

The word "Kloot" comes from Low German, which is closely related to Dutch, and means a clod or clump of earth. Balls of stone were later used, as were flint balls and iron balls weighing two pounds or one kilogram. The ultimate missile of choice was a sphere of wood from an apple tree filled with lead. Researchers believe that *Klootschiessen* was developed from the use of a Frisian weapon, with Frisian (freedom) fighters feared for their skill with projectiles. The object of the East Frisian version of the game is to throw the ball as far as possible after making the shortest possible run and jump from a ramp. The rules differentiate between a field version and a standing version. The field version is more traditional and played when there is frost on the ground. Two teams throw the ball across fields and meadows for a specific distance. This is usually about seven kilometres or four miles. The place where the ball eventually comes to rest marks the spot

where the next shot is taken. This is not the case with the standing version, where all participants play against one another. The winner is the person who hurls their ball the furthest. As in shot putting, the roll of the ball after it has landed is not counted. *Klootschiess* clubs tend to favour the standing version for tournaments and can play on conventional sports grounds or fields.

Klootschiessen also has its own book of records. The 100-metre or 330-foot mark was first reached by Gerd Gerdes in 1935. Nobody managed to throw their *Kloot* further for 50 years. In 1985 two men broke the record: Harm Henkel from Aurich threw his ball 102 metres (335 feet) and, funnily enough on exactly the same day, Hans-George Bohlken, the Bear of Ellens, managed 102.5 metres (336 feet). The current record is 106.2 metres (348 feet), set in 2006 by Stefan Albarus from Norden. He was undoubtedly driven to his success by his supporters shouting the *Klootschiessers'* self-chosen motto "Lüch up en fleu herut" or "Lift up and fly far!"

East Frisian jokes

"Why do East Frisians take the door off when they're in the bath? So that nobody can look through the keyhole". Like every other nation in the world, Germany loves a scapegoat to tell jokes about. For the north of the country, it's the East Frisians. In the 1960s and 1970s, jokes about East Frisians were something of a cult. And it's not as if the people who live between the western North Sea Coast, Oldenburg and the Emsland are annoyed about it. On the contrary: the region is actually credited with the invention and cultivation of the East Frisian joke. All share the same question-and-answer format. Usually the northeners bear the brunt of the joke but sometimes it's the Bavarians. Stand-up comedian Otto Waalkes has this one, for instance: "The East Frisian and the Bavarian football teams are playing a match. There's a railway line close to the stadium; a train passes and whistles. The East Frisians think the match is over and go home; half an hour later, Bavaria shoots the first goal."

As already mentioned, the East Frisian joke dates back to the 60s and 70s. It was the first in a national trend for themed jibes, such as those later aimed at blondes. As opposed to the latter, the East Frisian genre has a precise origin, namely the high school in Westerstede which many East Frisians have attended – and which is no longer in East Frisia. Local rivalries have also been the subject of jest, such as that between the East Frisians and the people of Ammerland, for example. This peaked in 1968 and 1969 in a series published by pupil Borwin Bandelow in the school Magazine *Der Trompeter* (The Trumpeter). Writing for the alleged *Research and Teaching* section, his 'scientific' articles centred on a clumsy and rather stupid species called *Homo ostfrisiensis*.

The series quickly spread throughout the region and later to the rest of what was then West Germany. Memorable reports were printed in renowned magazines such as *Stern* and *Spiegel* about the curious battle between *Ammerländer* and East Frisians; these often included jokes from and about North Germany. The true potential of the East Frisian joke only revealed itself a few years later. Comedy bards like Karl Dall, famous for his shows with Insterburg & Co. on Radio Bremen, and the aforementioned Otto Waalkes built their entire careers on the back of jokes about their East Frisian contemporaries. Even jazz singer Knut Kiesewetter earned a bit of extra cash recording discs of East Frisian jokes. The pioneer of this particular form of entertainment was East Frisian humorist and chansonnier Hannes Flesner who in 1971 issued several LPs of East Frisian jokes in an entire series devoted to the (affectionate) derision of his fellow countrymen.

East Frisia today

The East Frisians see themselves as something of a link between Germany and the Netherlands. For today, now that our European borders are open, many national discrepancies have paled into insignificance. Especially in places where the expanses of green countryside fail to indicate where one country ends and another starts, you may suddenly find yourself reading a sign saying "Welcome to the Netherlands".

The northwest, with its islands, wide, open country, and very special charm, is also a popular holiday destination. Families and cyclists in particular have been coming here for several decades now. The islands have long been second home to the population of North Rhein-Westphalia; the A31 motorway between the Ruhr and East Frisia was finished around ten years ago and provides a direct link from the industrial heart of the west to the surf and turf of the northwest.

This land on the coast is more modern than it has ever been, a commodity especially evident in the field of renewable energy. Where wind parks are only slowly taking hold in Bavaria and Baden-Württemberg, in East Frisia they have long been part of the scenery. Wind power is also one of several business sectors where East Frisia has become something of a locomotive for the future. Big-time wind turbine manufacturers such as Enercon, Bard and Enova assemble their giant power generators between Ems and Jadebusen – and in the very recent past have notched up commissions for offshore wind farms planned for the entire North Sea. Emden has long been an important base port in this field.

And then there's one of the largest and most successful shipyards in Europe: Meyer Werft. In Papenburg in the Emsland, which culturally and geographically separates East Frisia from its neighbours, ships and boats have been built since 1795. In the mid 1980s the Meyer shipyard, family owned since it was founded, began building the biggest cruise liners in the world – which now regularly travel down the River Ems to be launched at sea in Emden.

Page 22/23:
The old harbour in Emden is special in its own way. The town developed around its port, now officially a museum harbour full of wonderful old ships.

Page 24/25:
Evening light on the mudflats of Dollart Bay in the Rheiderland. This stretch of coastline is one of the four historic territories of East Frisia in the district of Leer. Part of the Rheiderland is in East Frisia, the other part in the Netherlands.

Age-old centres of trade:
the town of Emden and the Leer District

Leer lit up for Christmas. The building with the splendid tower is the town hall, with the historic weigh house next door.

Arriving in Emden you may gasp in amazement at the wonderful old ships moored in the harbour, many of them now floating museums. With a population of 52,000 Emden has much more than just ancient marine craft, however. The largest town in East Frisia is an age-old trading post with a historical centre and a tradition going back a good 1,300 years.

The town is in the district of Leer which boasts many old villages and hamlets. Emden and Leer are joined by a traditional yet unusual form of transport: the Ditzum ferry across the River Ems. For many decades this moving bridge has linked the village of Ditzum in Rheiderland, part of the Leer District, with the Emden suburb of Petkum. The Rheiderland and the other communities in the administrative district have retained their age-old charm. The ancient landscape of East Frisia comprises the Rheiderland in the west, Overledingerland in the southeast, Moormerland in the north and Lengenerland. They are carved into neat sections by perfectly straight ditches and canals once used not only to transport peat but also to drain the moors and bogs.

The district town is Leer, after Emden and Aurich the third-largest in East Frisia with 34,000 inhabitants. The old town in Leer is heralded as being the best in East Frisia, with no less than four castles, many patrician town dwellings and churches from several different centuries. Situated at the confluence of the Leda and Ems rivers, Leer is also an ancient trading post, one of Germany's largest shipping locations and seat of the Bünting Group, who are famous for their tea throughout Europe.

Above:

The Jann Berghaus Brücke over the River Ems at Leer is one of the oldest bascule bridges of its kind in Western Europe. It measures 464 metres (1,522 feet) and was built at the start of the 1990s when the Ems was widened and deepened so that ships from the Meyer shipyard could pass through this bottleneck.

Right:

Spectacles like this attract thousands of people every year. Like the Celebrity Eclipse, shown here, luxury cruise liners have to be towed along the Ems to Emden from the Meyer shipyard in Papenburg. This floating hotel has been in service in Europe and the Caribbean since April 2010.

Left:
The old town of Leer with its pedestrian zone is a local attraction, with its many historical houses forming a pretty backdrop.

Below:
No shipping town would be complete without a maritime college. Many attend the popular nautical science course at the university of applied sciences in Emden-Leer.

Right:

View of the old harbour in Weener which numbers just 16,000 inhabitants. Weener is in the Rheiderland and was once on the trade route to the south of the Münsterland. Trading, horse and livestock markets were once a frequent occurrence here but those days are long gone. Up until 1932 Weener was the seat of the local administrative district which is now Leer District.

Right:

This bronze statue by Karl-Ludwig Böke entitled Peat Women stands at the entrance to the harbour in Weener. It pays homage to the hard lives the people of East Frisia once led, digging peat to heat their modest homes.

Far right:

Fronehaus is the oldest house in Weener, erected in 1660. It has a typical Renaissance gable and is still used as a private home.

Right page:

A symbol of patriotism from a past age: this statue of Germania in Weener is a memorial to the fallen men of the town who died during the Franco-Prussian War of 1870/1871.

page:
ndorp Church in
ngum is one of the
ion's neoclassical
ces of worship built in
ck, erected in 1820.
e chancel inside is from
previous 17th-century
Iding. The roof of the
ve is held up by wooden
rrel vaulting and the
urch organist plays on
ührer organ from 1963.

The reformed St Sixtus
Church is the local land-
mark of Jemgum, its
steeple shaped like a lighthouse. The church has a
turbulent history; it was
refurbished several times
and had to be completely
rebuilt following fires in
1930 and 2004.

Like the church in Jemgum
the one in Ditzum also
has a lighthouse-shaped
bell tower. The church was
probably constructed
between 1180 and 1220 on
a man-made mound and
has been refurbished
several times in the course
of its history. The separate
steeple at the west end
was added in 1846 by
Marten Bruns Schmidt.
In 2009 the bells were
restored, including one
from 1479.

Left:
The Ditzum ferry over the Ems is a must for tourists. It was also often used by commuters on their way to work in the big towns.

Below left:
This view out across the harbour in Ditzum is typical of East Frisia. Shrimp cutters and shrimp fishing are still an important pillar of the local economy. The windmills were once erected to drain the land, among other uses.

Below:
The Ditzum ferry across the Ems moored in the harbour at Ditzum. The small boat joins Ditzum and the Emden suburb of Petkum. Where it was once an essential form of transport for the people who worked at the Nordsee-Werken in Emden, today it's primarily used by cyclists doing one of the three local routes here: the International Dollard Route, the Dortmund-Ems Canal Route and the North Sea Coast Trail.

Page 36/37:
En route from the Meyer shipyard in Papenburg to the North Sea, one of the small ports the big cruise liners pass is Ditzum. Here, the Aidasol.

FAMOUS EAST FRISIANS

With jokes about the East Frisians something of a cult in Germany, it's hardly surprising that this bit of the country should have produced some of the greats of German comedy, their humour ranging from slapstick to biting sarcasm – and always spiced with a hefty portion of self-irony. Otto Waalkes is one, born in Emden in 1948. The young man took his first creative steps in the field of music as a member of a beat band called The Rustlers. After passing his A levels the shy East Frisian went to Hamburg to study art. In order to earn a bit of extra money he began playing the trendy clubs and bars of Hamburg. Otto says he owes his later career as a comedian to his clumsiness; while reeling off his repertoire of songs by Lee Marvin he often managed to knock over his stool or microphone – which generated more applause than his singing did. In 1985 the East Frisian hit the cinema screens. His first film was *Otto – The Movie*; three more followed. His films were seen by an estimated 25 million. He now spends little of his time in Emden.

Karl Dall was also born in Emden in 1941. He has made a name for himself not only as a comedian but also as a TV presenter, singer and actor. His trademark, a dropping right eyelid, is caused by a weak muscle.

Dall rose to fame through his work with Ingo Insterburg, Jürgen Barz and Peter Ehlebracht. In 1967 they founded the group Insterburg & Co which existed until the end of the 1970s. From 1985 to 1991 Karl Dall indulged his provocative side in his own talk show *Dall As*. He is recorded as having once said to German pop singer Roland Kaiser, "OK, now sing so that we've got it over and done with." The singer promptly walked out. A big milestone in Karl Dall's career was his role as a chaotic film presenter and hoax caller in the hidden camera show *Verstehen Sie Spaß?* which he hosted with Kurt Felix and Paola from 1983 to 1990. In 2005 he again started performing with Ingo Insterburg.

Journalist and art collector
Henri Nannen is one of the greatest personalities of German post-war journalism. As a publisher, long-term editor in chief and editor of Stern magazine Nannen, who was born in Emden in 1913 and died in Hamburg in 1996,

influenced several generations of journalists. During the Second World War he was a war reporter and in 1946 he ended up in Hanover where he was granted a licence by the British occupying forces, founding the *Hannoversche Neueste Nachrichten* daily newspaper which he edited until 1947. Nannen was then editor in chief of the *Hannoversche Abendpost*. His greatest commercial success was when in 1948 he set up the illustrated magazine *Stern*. In 1951 he sold his shares to printer Richard Gruner and to the weekly newspaper *Die Zeit* run by Gerd Bucerius.

From 1949 to 1980 Henri Nannen was *Stern*'s editor in chief and its managing editor from 1983 onwards. During this period *Stern* was the magazine with the biggest print run in Europe yet while in office Nannen also had to answer to the scandal surrounding the forged Hitler diaries. Consistent as ever he accused himself of neglecting his duties as a journalist. In 1985 he endowed an award for journalism which is now known as the Henri Nannen Prize. Over the years the editor put together a valuable art collection which he donated to his home town of Emden on his 70th birthday. A special art gallery was built for this purpose and opened in 1986. In 1989 Henri Nannen was made an honorary citizen of Emden; his third wife Eske Nannen is now the gallery manager.

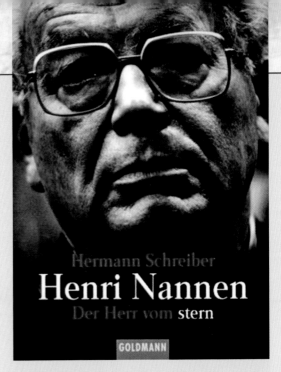

Right:
One of the great German journalists of the 20th century is Henri Nannen. He was one of the founders of Stern magazine and an avid collector of works of art, later bequeathing his entire collection to his native town of Emden. This now forms the basis of the Emden art gallery.

Left:
This bronze statue of famous pirate Klaus Störtebecker can be found in Marienhafe. It was fashioned by sculptor Karl-Ludwig Böke from Leer from the etching of Störtebecker by Daniel Hopfner. The pirate is said to have stayed in the village from 1396 to 1400.

Right:
Otto Waalkes is probably one of the most famous East Frisians today. Waalkes grew up in Emden and studied in Hamburg, where his talents as a comedian were accidentally discovered.

Far left:
In Knock, which is part of Emden, there is a statue of Friedrich Wilhelm von Brandenburg. In erecting it the East Frisians have paid homage to the Great Elector for clearing the land for farming.

Right:
Karl Dall, the man with the drooping eyelid from Emden, rose to fame in the 1970s with comics Insterburg & Co. After the group disbanded Dall embarked on a successful solo career and is still going strong.

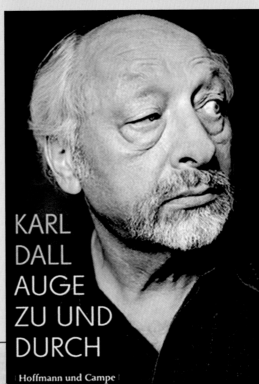

This page:
East Frisia is not only home to the locals and – for part of the year at least – tourists. Many have made themselves a new home here, like this one belonging to a couple from Unna in the northwest of Germany.

Page 42/43:
The River Ems flows into the Dollart at Emden. The eastern edge of this wide bay belongs to Germany, with the western shore part of the Netherlands. Like Jadebusen, Dollart Bay was formed by the great storm tides of the Middle Ages.

Right pag
*Wybelsum Polder is one
East Frisia's biggest wi
farms. Beneath the wi
turbines busy produci
electricity for the loc
populace, the she
contentedly munch on t
lush grass of the s
marshe*

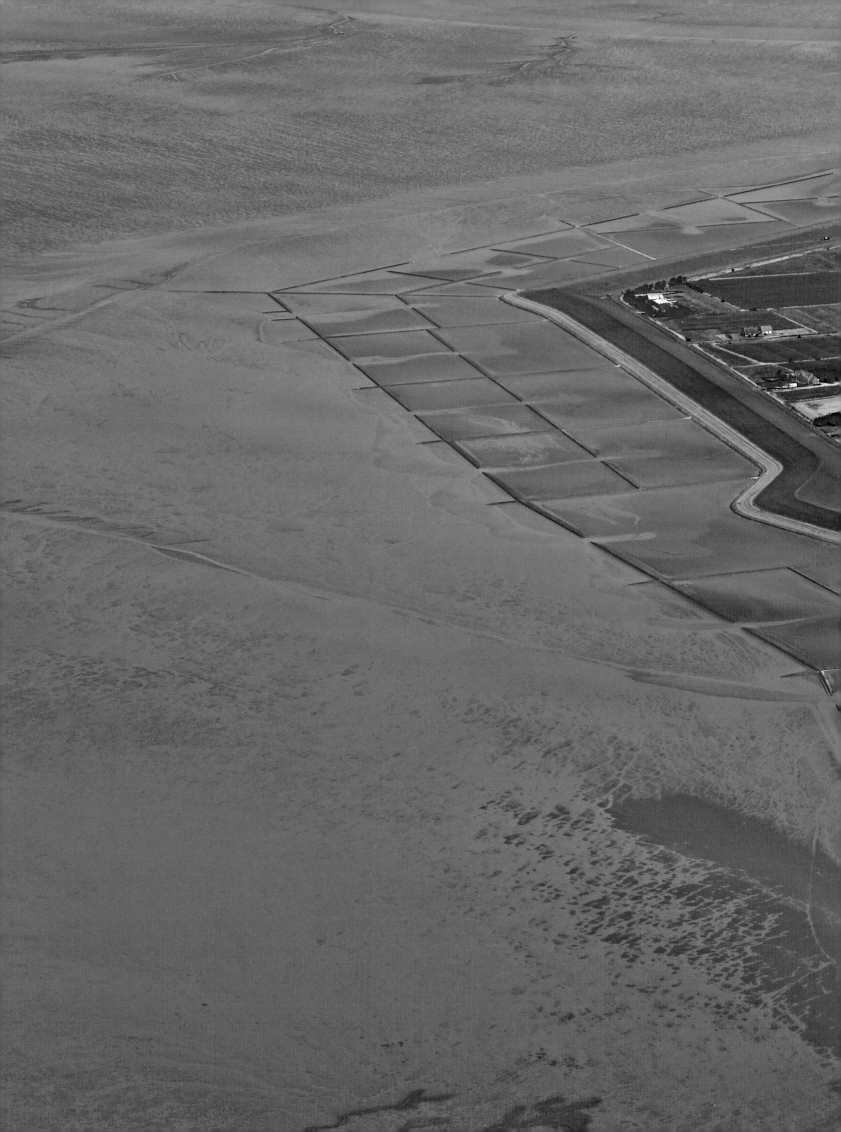

Right:
The Rheiderland is absolutely typical of East Frisia, with hardly any elevations interrupting the flat landscape. Sunrise and sunset are particularly beautiful here.

Left:
Ship in Dollart Bay. Despite its size large ships have to be guided along the Ems Estuary as the shipping channel is narrow and has to be constantly redug, as shown here. In the background is Delfzijl in the Netherlands.

The Rheiderland is divided up by canals and ditches as straight as a ruler. They bear mute witness to the endeavours of past generations to drain the land and make it suitable for farming.

Right:
The Norwegian flag being flown outside the town hall in Emden for the harbour festival, a mark of the town's international character.

Far right:
Detail of the harbour archway in Emden. It demonstrates how rich the town once was through its trade with the whole of Europe.

Right page:
Flat-bottomed boats in the harbour in Emden illustrate that the East Frisian metropolis was the main centre of trade for all parts of the region. The water here was flat and could only be navigated by boats without a keel rump.

Right:
Little fish seller Jantje Vis stands at the entrance to the harbour in Emden. The statue was erected in 1986 and reminds us that Emden once had one of the biggest fleets of herring luggers in Europe.

Far right:
This anchor in the harbour at Emden reminds us of the sailors of old. The men once went aboard their ships in the centre of town; the port has now been moved to deeper water.

Left page:
Life at sea had very little to do with the romantic images conjured up by various songs, as visitors to the museum ships in Emden will soon discover. Emden's town hall can be seen in the background, situated at the main port of call in East Frisia's largest 'city'.

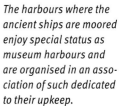

The harbours where the ancient ships are moored enjoy special status as museum harbours and are organised in an association of such dedicated to their upkeep.

Many an old seadog likes to spend his retirement aboard one of the old museum ships, either his own or one where he was part of the crew that manned it.

Page 52/53:
In the run up to Christmas Emden is aglow with festive lights. The Christmas market is held around the old harbour and is said to be one of the prettiest in Germany.

On the North Coast:
the districts of Aurich and Wittmund

Aurich seen from above, with the harbour on the left. In the past the second-largest town in East Frisia was the seat of East Frisia's princes and frequently the centre of administration – as it still is. This tradition has earned Aurich the nickname of "the secret capital of East Frisia".

This is where the waves crash against the shore, with the ocean stretching to the horizon and beyond and the air fresh with the briny smell of the North Sea. The district of Aurich is famous for its communities of Krummhörn with Greetsiel Beach, Norden, Hagermarsch and Dornum. The coastline continues with Holtgast, Esens, Neuharlingersiel and a thin slither of Wittmund. The latter are in the Wittmund District, as are the two East Frisian Islands of Langeoog and Spiekeroog. Juist, Norderney and Baltrum, on the other hand, are part of Aurich District.

Especially in summer, when tourists flock to the coast or set sail in their thousands for one of the beautiful East Frisian Islands, much of public life takes place outdoors along the coastline of the North Sea. Here you can wade through the Wattenmeer or Wadden Sea for miles, admire the pretty coastal resorts and enjoy the many activities these have to offer. For those interested in the history of East Frisia there is plenty to discover in the annals of the Aurich and Wittmund districts. According to research the Harlingerland, the stretch of land on the North Sea Coast that includes much of the area around Esens and Wittmund, deserves a special place in the history of the region. When Frisia was divided into its many independent districts or lands Harlingerland was known as Herloga and probably formed in the middle of the 11th century from parts of the old tribal gaus of Nordwidu and Wanga.

Photos, left:
View from the pedestrian zone in Aurich of the Lambertiturm, Aurich's local landmark, 35 metres (115 feet) high. The steeple was built in the 14th century and has since been extended many times. The last extensive restoration was in 1994/95. The nave is from 1833 to 1835 and replaces the previous hall church. Every evening at 9 pm the bells ring out the distinctive tune of Rüm-Straat-Lüden.

Left page:
The Knodtsches Haus in Aurich, named after its long-term owner lawyer Knodt, was built in the Dutch late baroque style in c. 1735. The house initially belonged to royal master builder Heinrich Horst.

Left:
The market place in Aurich is a popular place to meet. Children like to play in the fountain here, especially in summer.

Right:

Aurich's pretty Kirchstrasse. One of its more traditional buildings is the Ostfriesische Nachrichten building, a newspaper that has been published since 1864. It's the most widely read local rag in Aurich and the environs and comes with the Neue Osnabrücker Nachrichten as its main paper.

Far right:

The tower of Aurich's palace. The present ensemble stands on the site of an old moated castle, the seat of the tribal Cirksena family. It was built in 1447 and fell into disrepair over the following centuries. King Georg V of Hanover had the present edifice built between 1851 and 1855; it's now home to Lower Saxony's salaries and pensions office.

Right:

Medicines are still sold where the locals once came for their tinctures and remedies – some more effective than others. The royal apothecary on Burgstrasse in Aurich was opened in 1433. Its long tradition is occasionally celebrated by the present occupiers on special historic pharmacy days.

The Schwarzer Bär or black bear was once one of the oldest inns in Aurich, first mentioned in 1691. In 1802 the members of the Literarische Ressource or literary resource reading circle met here and in later years the tavern was also a cinema. Now only its façade reminds us of its original purpose.

The old church hall belonging to the Lamberti parish. This is still the largest parish in Aurich and organises a number of activities.

Page 60/61:
Count Edzard Cirksena II moved his seat of government from Emden to Aurich in 1561. These royal stables were built in 1587 and completely redesigned in the 18th century. The building is now symmetrical with an entrance and stairs on both sides of the arcade with its 14 pillars.

Right:
When it turns cold the East Frisians devote themselves to their national sport: Klootschiessen. This is like the form of boules played all over North Germany. The object of the game is to hurl a ball as far as you can across a fixed distance. Fields, meadows and also public roads are used as the 'pitch'.

Below:
The Upstalsboom on a hill in Rahe near Aurich is inextricably linked to the history of East Frisia. In the Middle Ages this is where East Frisian leaders met and held court. The Upstalsboom is now chiefly a tourist site.

The moorland museum in Aurich-Walle illustrates the poor conditions people once lived in. This clay hut from 1924 shows how the peat farmers of East Frisia eked out their meagre existence, the course of the year largely determined by the forces of nature.

Left:
Wiesmoor is almost as famous for its flowers as it is for its peat. The heat generated when the peat was burned in the former power station was used to cultivate plants. The power plant is now history but local gardening expertise is still very much in evidence, the decorative produce of which can be admired in the flower hall.

Below:
The flower hall and surrounding area make up the Blumenreich gardens which entice countless gardening enthusiasts to Wiesmoor every year.

The museum of local history in Wiesmoor also demonstrates that life here was harsh and very simple. People used to live in estate houses such as this one (above). Goods were transported along the canals in barges which were sometimes towed but usually had sails (right). Bread was baked in the bakehouse. Sited away from the main farm building there was less danger of possible fires spreading from the oven to the house. Buckets and milk churns could be turned upside down to dry on the wooden frame outside (far right).

Left:
This bedroom in the museum in Wiesmoor shows visitors just how cramped conditions were.

Left:
Settlers on the fens also used bicycles to get about, with a carbide lamp to light the way at night.

Far left:
The utensils people needed to make food are on display in the museum kitchen in Wiesmoor. There wasn't much space here, either.

Left:
Children were taught at small village schools. The girls and boys first had to take their wooden clogs off before studying the three R's under the stern gaze of the schoolmaster.

A flat-bottomed boat on one of the many canals near Grossefehn. Flat-bottomed boats don't have a keel and can thus sail in shallow water.

Like in the Alps of Switzerland there are places in East Frisia where jobs still have to be done by hand. One of these is scything patches of wild grass close to the canal.

Right page:
Bagband Mill in Grossefehn, a smock windmill built in 1812. Up until 1910 the mill had sailcloth sails, with slatted sails replacing them in 1911.

East Frisian cooking: simple yet substantial

Our eating habits over the past half a century have definitely gone global – and East Frisia is no exception. However, there are still many dishes which are more or less typical of the Ems/Jade/Dollart region. The local cuisine is like the countryside: a little meagre and simple but attractive, substantial and nutritional.

The East Frisians love pork – which is why menus include things like the strange-sounding *Sniertjebraa*. After schnitzel this must be the most popular meat dish in the area. To make it cooks use fresh pork schnitzel cut up into bits, to which onions and flour are added. The tasty pork pieces are served with red cabbage, beetroot, pickled gherkins and potatoes. Another delicious method of preparation for the domestic pig is *Glühweinbraten* or mulled wine roast which tastes especially good after a game or two of *Klootschiessen* or East Frisian *boules*. It's thus eaten when it's cold outside, namely from the end of October or the beginning of November. The pork is rubbed with a mixture of salt, pepper, pimento, rosemary, bayleaf and thyme. After the meat has been braised in spiced wine for one or two hours, it's served with pears.

But if you think East Frisian cooking is all pork, you're wrong. There are enough sheep running about on the dykes for one or two to be sacrificed for human consumption. Incidentally, only young lambs are slaughtered; the meat of older sheep is simply too tough. East Frisian lamb has a very special taste as the animals have spent their short lives grazing on salt marshes. Roast lamb from Extum is one such delicacy. If you want to prepare it yourself, you may need some practice as its strong aroma means that you have to go easy on the herbs and spices. Before the leg of lamb is roasted, the fat is removed and the lamb spiced with garlic. It's cooked with a mixture of vegetables put in a marinade the night before which includes beans, onions, carrots, bayleaf, pimento, parsley and tomatoes. The cooked roast is served with bread.

Fish is of course also a frequent item on the menu, including fried fresh herring and 'green' eel. The latter is not a specific marine species but common eel turned 'green' by its accompaniments of dill and boiled potatoes. There are also less carnivorous delights to be tried, including East Frisian grey peas with bacon,

Updrögt or dried beans and Rheiderland potato soup. A thick slice of East Frisian tart goes down well as a dessert.

The land of tea

Like England, East Frisia would be lost without its tea. Practically nowhere else in Germany drinks as much of it as the northwest. Did we say "drink"?! That's something of an understatement. In East Frisia tea isn't merely drunk; it's celebrated in an elaborate tea ceremony.

People generalise when they talk about East Frisian tea. The tea isn't of course actually grown here; what's meant is a blend of many different types of tea, most of them from Assam. To this Java, Ceylon, Sumatra and Darjeeling blends are added; a good East Frisian tea contains at least ten different varieties. The ceremony begins when the kettle has boiled and the cream and candied sugar lumps or *Kluntjes* have been put on the table.

The secret to a good brew lies in the preparation. First the sugar is put in the cup, then the tea is poured in. The cream is allowed to dribble slowly off the cream spoon down the inside edge of the cup. The cold cream sinks and then swirls back up to the surface like a miniature cloud. The tea is thus drunk in three stages; first you taste the mild cream, then the slightly bitter tea and finally the sweet sugar.

The East Frisian ceremony requires quite a bit of equipment: the obligatory teapot and teacups, a special East Frisian teaspoon, a teapot warmer, a tea strainer for the cup or spout and the *Rohmlepel* or cream spoon. The tea should be strong and the water soft. Hard water would be totally unauthentic and threaten the success of this holy ceremony...

Left:
Shrimp cutter in the harbour at Neuharlingersiel. The delicious shellfish are something of a basic foodstuff here on the coast.

Above:
Matjes or filleted herring and fried potatoes are on of the most popular dishe on the coast. East Frisia is no exception, with this hearty North German delicacy found on any sel respecting menu.

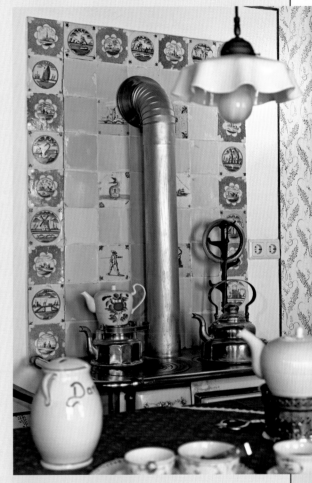

Top right:
One regional tradition associated with the New Year are these special cones no East Frisian could imagine doing without when the bells ring out the old and the fireworks start.

Centre right:
The tea cult in East Frisia doesn't only centre on the beverage itself but also on its preparation. This wonderful tea kitchen can be found at the tea museum in Norden.

Right:
The tea museum in Norden is devoted to the East Frisian tea cult. It traces the history of the brew from its origins to the present day.

71

Right

Suurhus church in the parish of Hinte is in the Guinness Book of Records as the most crooked tower in the world – even more wonky than the Leaning Tower of Pisa. The semi-fortified church was built on a man-made mound in the middle of the 13th century.

Right:

This sandstone lion adorns the castle of Hinta in the village of Hinte.

Far right:

This dovecote can also be found in the grounds of Burg Hinta.

Right page:

The castle of Hinta stands in the centre of Hinte village and dates back to the 13th century. It took on its present form following several periods of refurbishment in the 18th and 19th centuries.

Right:
Rysum with its pretty church is 15 kilometres or 9 miles west of Emden. The entire village has been built on a circular man-made mound just 400 metres or 1,300 feet across. The village and its population of 700 were made part of Krummhörn in 1972.

Far right:
Another of East Frisia's splendid organs can be found in the church in Rysum. This instrument is from the mid 15th century and one of the oldest organs in the world that can still be played.

Right:
Manningaburg in the heart of Pewsum was erected by the tribal Manniga family in 1458. Both Pewsum and the castle fell to the Cirksena nobles in 1565. The castle is now part of the East Frisian Open-Air Museum.

Right page:
The lighthouse in Campen, which was officially opened on October 1, 1891, is still Germany's tallest lighthouse at 65.3 metres or 214.2 feet. It stands at the mouth of the Ems northwest of Emden and acts as a landmark and sector light. Its design is extremely unusual, its free-standing steel frame triangular in plan and the steps running up a giant pipe at its centre.

Page 76/77:
Where sailors use the lighthouse in Campen for navigation, less seaworthy visitors can enjoy the spectacular views from the top.

East Frisia is also pretty in the winter. The church in Eilsum looks especially romantic with its frosted trees, while the sheep seem to blend in with the snow, distinguished only by their baaing. The areas close to Pilsum lighthouse and the twin windmills in Greetsiel are also magical in their winter cloak of white.

Top left page:
Greetsiel with its population of ca. 1,500 is part of Krummhörn and goes back over 650 years. One of the village's mainstays, apart from tourism, has always been fish and shrimp fishing. The harbour is linked to the sea by a lock on the Leybuchthörn, a spit of land that juts out into the Wadden Sea.

This roof turret adorns the Reformed Protestant church in Greetsiel. The place of worship was built in two stages between 1380 and 1410 and was once the private chapel of chieftain Haro Edzardsna. The church steeple has been built slightly away from the main building.

These old tombstones outside the nave show visitors how far back the Reformed church in Greetsiel goes. Pope Boniface IX recognised the building as a church in 1401. The first organ was installed in 1555, the last – still played – in 1963.

Bottom left page:
The houses on the harbour bear witness to the history of Greetsiel. The village was where the Cirksena family came from, the tribal chieftains who were counts and princes of East Frisia between 1654 and 1744. Greetsiel was first mentioned in 1388.

Page 82/83:
In the distance the village
of Pilsum, the church and
a wind turbine rise up
from the flat landscape
where you can see today
who's coming to visit
tomorrow, as a local
saying goes.

Warnfried Church from the
12th century is one of the
sights in the little village
of Osteel. The church is
dedicated to St Werenfried
and boasts the second
oldest organ in East Frisia.
Osteel also has a monu-
ment to astronomer
Johannes Fabricius.

*There are a few small
towns in East Frisia which
have their own palace.
One of them is Dornum
with its moated castle
of Norderburg, shown
here with its Christmas
decorations.*

Above:
East Frisia has plenty to offer in the way of scenery. This nature protection area near Greetsiel is run by the German Nature and Biodiversity Conservation Union and has a hive for the observation of local birds and animals.

Right:
(Re)claiming land has always been an important topic in East Frisia. People once battled with the sea in order to gain land for habitation and farming; now endeavours are largely targeted towards putting right the damage done by storm tides which are becoming ever fiercer in the wake of the climate change.

Schloss Lütetsburg east of the town of Norden is surrounded by a splendid park. It was built in 1212 by Lütet Manninga from Westeel. After the village was swallowed by a heavy storm tide in the Leybucht in 1373 the castle was extended. It was later destroyed during the Saxon Feud of 1514 and rebuilt between 1557 and 1576. The palace, owned by the counts of Innhausen and Knyphausen, also burned down several times, the last time being in 1956. By 1960 Schloss Lütetsburg had been rebuilt on the foundations of its predecessors in a more modern fashion. The palace park is open to the public and in 2009 two nine-hole golf courses were added.

The German Maritime Search and Rescue Service:
unsung heroes

Adolph Bermpohl just wouldn't accept it. The navigation instructor, who first taught at the maritime college in Vegesack and later in Emden and Bremen and who lived from 1833 to 1887, was scandalised by the Right of Salvage that decreed that anything washed onto land by the sea was the property of the person who found it. For smallholders and fishermen this was a valuable source of supplementary income and they often had little interest in saving those in trouble at sea – which in those days was a frequent occurrence. On the contrary: ships were allowed to run aground and sailors to drown while those in relative safety on land simply went down to the beach to collect the spoils.

This was again the case on September 10, 1860. The brig *Alliance* had become caught on the notorious reef offshore from the East Frisian Island of Borkum. Nine seamen lost their lives. Adolph Bermpohl heard of the tragic accident and in the weeks following the incident lamented in the weekly *Wochenschrift für Vegesack und Umgegend* that there were no facilities for saving those in distress at sea. Bermpohl was also speaking from experience, having been the victim of a maritime accident himself in 1849.

In 1860 Bermpohl thus called for the establishing of "rescue stations on the German North Sea Islands" in a number of newspaper articles. The setup was to be a private organisation not funded by the state, with work performed by volunteers. Three years later Bermpohl was instrumental in the founding of the Bremen Association for the Rescue of the Shipwrecked which was to be one of the forerunners of the German Maritime Search and Rescue Service or DGzRS founded in Kiel in 1865, which is still based in Bremen.

800 volunteers and 2,000 missions a year
Not much has changed in the basic setup of Germany's sea rescue service. Along the North and Baltic coasts the safety of shipping routes and the coastline in general is ensured by 185 full-time employees and over 800 volunteers operating 61 modern rescue cruisers and lifeboats, stationed from the Ems Estuary – the westernmost lifeboat station is on the island of Borkum – to Stettiner Haff, with the network's easternmost point in Ueckermünde. Missions range from sav-

ing people's lives at sea to evacuating the sick from ships or islands to the mainland to technical aid and firefighting. The search and rescue teams run over 2,000 missions a year. So that this is possible about 600 volunteer workers are at work throughout the country supporting the lifeboat service, with some even based in the neighbouring countries of Austria and Switzerland. The DGzRS still operates as a charity.

Since its founding the technology and equipment used by the rescuers has completely changed. At the outset the service was operated by brave men who launched rowing boats into the churning waves from their rescue station on the beach. Close to the coast rubber rings with canvas trousers sewn onto them were later installed, as were rocket-powered towlines which could be fired out to stranded ships. In 1911 the first motorised boats were used. Today's watercraft, in all classes from seven to 46 metres in length (23 to 150 feet), are distinguished by the fact that they are built of aluminium. All of them are capsize-proof; should they be turned upside down in a stormy sea, they automatically right themselves.

Maritime search and rescue is managed by the Maritime Rescue Coordination Centre or MRCC, who not only coordinate missions run by the DGzRS fleet but also the air rescue services operated by German Navy helicopters as part of international Search and Rescue (SAR). State-of-the-art technology even makes it possible to bring rescue missions on the other side of the world to a happy conclusion with the help of Germany's unsung maritime heroes.

Left:
The Neuharlingersiel lifeboat is named after its home port on the North Sea Coast. Ten volunteers are on call to go out with the boat, built at Schweers in Bardenfleth in 2000.

Above:
When it was in service thi boat was known as the Walther Müller but was renamed the Eppe de Bloo in 2006. In March 2007 it was decommissioned and now guards the old lifeboat station in Dornumersiel.

Small photos, right, from top to bottom: At 46 metres or 150 feet in length the Hermann Marwede maritime rescue cruiser is currently the largest in the fleet operated by the German Maritime Search and Rescue Service or DGzRS. It is stationed at Helgoland.

The DGzRS is also active in the extreme east of Germany, such as in Ueckermünde on the Stettiner Haff. This rigid hull inflatable boat, the Dora, has been specially customized for this region and is 6.8 metres or 22 feet long.

The 23.1-metre or 76-foot maritime rescue cruiser Bernhard Gruben is stationed on Norderney. The ship was constructed in 1997 at the Schweers shipyard in Bardenfleth on the Lower Weser; the sister boat is called Johann Fidi.

The Cassen Knigge lifeboat in the harbour of Norddeich. It was built in 1993 at the Fassmer shipyard in Berne-Motzen. The Cassen Knigge is 8.5 metres or 28 feet long.

Right page:
The lively centre of Esens with its pedestrianised zone is popular with locals and tourists alike.

The district of Esens is governed from the town hall here in Esens. The area was officially created in 1972 during Lower Saxony's reform of the administrative districts yet the origins of the town itself date back to the year 800. Esens was first mentioned in 1310 as Eselingis.

This dancing bear in Esens commemorates a medieval legend. In it the town was once again being besieged by enemy troops who were trying to starve the people of Esens into submission. When the situation became so dire that capitulation was imminent, a dancing bear belonging to a travelling minstrel broke free. Extremely hungry, he climbed to the top of one of the towers and started bombarding the besiegers with stones. They wrongly concluded that if the Esens had enough food to feed the bear then continuing the siege was fruitless. The army thus withdrew and Esens was saved.

Page 94/95:
Shrimp cutters waiting for their next trip out to sea in the harbour in Neuharlingersiel. The fishermen often sell their catch straight off the boat – advising customers that the shrimp have not yet been peeled.

Right:
Neuharlingersiel is opposite the two islands of Langeoog and Spiekeroog. This building with its rooftop restaurant at the mouth of the harbour is popular with locals and visitors.

Below:
The bronze statues at the end of the harbour in Neuharlingersiel commemorate the fact that the town has been a deep-sea fishing port since its first mention in 1693.

Above:
The Sielhof is one of the most distinctive buildings in Neuharlingersiel, erected in 1755 by Siebelt Frerichs Eymen. After changing hands the building was extensively restored between 1899 and 1906. The ground floor is now used as a restaurant.

Left:
This is a common scene in summer when holiday-makers wait in the harbour for their passage across the North Sea. Neuharlinger-siel chiefly serves the two East Frisian Islands of Spiekeroog and Langeoog.

Left page:
Carolinensiel, founded in 1730, is one of several museum ports on Germany's North Sea and Baltic coasts. The array of flat-bottomed boats is well worth seeing.

Left:
At the harbour museum visitors can learn about the history of the coast and about old ship and boatbuilding techniques – and of course how people spent their lives on and with the North Sea.

Photos, left:
Building wooden boots is still an art in itself. The people who have chosen this profession not only know how to make the boat actually float but are also versed in the artistic adornment of their marine craft.

Page 100/101:
Carolinensiel is also pretty in the run up to Christmas with its fairy lights and floating Christmas tree.

The church of St Florian's is in Funnix which is part of the town of Wittmund. The rectangular, hall-like edifice has a free-standing clock tower from the 13th century. In 2007 St Florian's became one of the churches here with regular opening times, enabling tourists to plan their visits and not be left standing outside closed doors.

St Mauritius in Reepsholt.
The Romanesque church
was constructed in c. 1200.
The steeple was added
in the 14th century but
collapsed in 1474 during
a siege on Reepholt. The
ruined tower is a local
landmark.

Page 104/105:
The pedestrianised zone
in Wittmund, the district
town. The district only
gained official access to
the North Sea during a
local government reform
when Carolinensiel was
made part of the town. The
main shopping street,
shown here, is a popular
port of call.

The local court in Wittmund. The present building dates back to 1872.

If Hollywood can do it, so can Wittmund! This little East Frisian town has its own Hands of Fame walk, where Hardy Krüger, Uwe Seeler, Christian Wulff and various other famous people have left their handprints in the tarmac.

This group of figures can also be found in the centre of Wittmund. The shepherd with his dog and sheep reminds us that land can't be successfully reclaimed without these woolly animals. Sheep grazing the dykes ensure that the grass stays short and compact, thus reinforcing the overall structure.

Right page:
Jever is famous for its beer, Jever Pils. The towers of the Friesian Jever Brewery are now a local landmark.

Right:
From 1428 onwards the palace in Jever was built on the foundations of an old castle, with extensive refurbishment carried out between 1560 and 1564. The palace was once the seat of the rulers of Jever.

Far right:
By some strange quirk of history Catherine the Great, empress of Russia, also ruled over East Frisia. Her portrait hangs in the audience chamber in the palace in Jever.

Right:
Jever is an old East Frisian centre of trade. Many buildings corroborate this fact, such as this warehouse in the old part of town.

Far right:
One of the most magnificent buildings in Jever is the local courthouse, marked by a statue of Justice on the roof.

108

The East Frisian Islands

Langeoog is one of the East Frisian Islands. The isle is 20 square kilometres or eight square miles in area and a popular holiday destination. Visitors love the long, sandy beach and mountainous sand dunes, some up to 20 metres or 66 feet tall.

No less than seven isles make up the chain of the East Frisian Islands: Borkum, Juist, Norderney, Baltrum, Langeoog, Spiekeroog and Wangerooge. The group also includes four uninhabited islets which are conservation areas: Lütje Hörn east of Borkum, Memmert with the Kachelotplate sandbank southwest of Juist, Minsener Oog southeast of Wangerooge and the bird reserve of Mellum Island.

The islands lie within a distance of 90 kilometres (56 miles) between the mouth of the River Ems and the Jade and Weser and are between 3.5 and ten kilometres (2 and 6 miles) offshore. The East Frisian Islands all have one thing in common: the side facing the mainland is lapped by the tides of the Wattenmeer or Wadden See, a natural habitat that is absolutely unique. The other side, looking out onto the open sea, is lined with fantastic sandy beaches.

The people here live with the sea. It provides both the fishing and tourist industries with a valuable source of income and helps to feed the thousands of guests who visit the islands, their resorts and their beaches year in, year out. People from the mainland first discovered the beauty and charm of the isles in the second half of the 19th century. Since then there has been much on offer to visitors, from the classic seaside holiday to various cultural events to spa treatments 365 days a year.

Guests greatly enjoy the islands which with their more sedate pace are in full keeping with the current trend for recuperation and stress management. Life here is all the more peaceful as cars are banned from all islands except Borkum – apart from emergency vehicles and the voluntary island fire brigades. Petrol and diesel fumes are taboo, with traffic consisting of electric cars, horse-drawn carriages and an ever increasing number of bicycles.

The Grosse Kaap is one of the three historic beacons on Borkum. It was erected together with the Kleines Kaap and Westkaap after the Franco-Prussian War in 1872 and helped guide ships into the Ems Estuary.

Impossible to miss with its bold red-and-white stripes, this lighthouse on Borkum stands on top of a high sand dune on the southwest side of the island. The lighthouse was erected in 1888/89 and was a sector light until it was taken out of service in the summer of 2003.

At 17 kilometres or 10 ½ miles in length Juist is the longest of the East Frisian Islands but only one kilometre or just over half a mile at its widest point. Its narrowest point measures 500 metres or 1,640 feet. Part of the Aurich district, 1,700 people live on the island, distributed between the main town of Juist and the Loog.

Juist is ju(i)st like the other East Frisian Islands in that its seaward side has beautiful sandy beaches and its inland flank opens out onto the unique habitat of the Wadden Sea.

Above:
Like all of the North Sea Coast Juist is popular with sailors and water sports fanatics. Skippers have to be skilled, though, as even near the islands the North Sea can be extremely dangerous.

Above left:
Memertfeuer is one of the sights on Juist. The lighthouse, which once stood on the neighbouring isle of Memmert, was shut down in 1986.

Left:
Cars are taboo here, as they are on almost all of the East Frisian Islands. For centuries the people of Juist have relied on old-fashioned horse power to conduct their daily business.

Above:
There are regular ferries from Norddeich to the island of Norderney. The tiny harbours dotted along the North Sea Coast are a vital link for the islanders.

Right:
Arriving in the little harbour on Norderney aboard a ferry is a fun experience whatever the time of year. Children especially like to watch the crew load and unload the cars and lorries.

Left:
At a good 26 square kilometres or 10 square miles Norderney is the second largest East Frisian Island after Borkum. It has a population of 5,800 and was made a town in 1848. Eighty-five percent of Norderney belongs to the Lower Saxony Wadden Sea National Park.

Below:
View of Norderney from the Wadden Sea where the 19th and 20th centuries are architecturally juxtaposed.

Above:
The hot favourite with visitors to Norderney is of course the beach – whatever the weather.

Right:
The East Frisian Islands wouldn't be the East Frisian Islands without their distinctive wicker beach chairs. Seaside visitors to Norderney are sure to ensconce themselves in one for the day.

Above:
Marienhöhe Restaurant is situated on the dune of the same name and is one of the more historic buildings on the island. The establishment is very close to the prom.

Far left:
Georgshöhe is one of the sandy elevations on the island. Atop it is a memorial to those who have lost their lives at sea.

Left:
Norderney's rehab clinic has been helping people overcome their health problems for many decades. The bracing North Sea climate is particularly beneficial to the treatment of respiratory diseases.

119

Left page:
Like all the other East Frisian Islands Norderney also has a church parish, theirs being Lutheran. East Frisia's church registry first listed a church on the island in 1420.

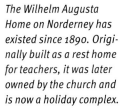

The Wilhelm Augusta Home on Norderney has existed since 1890. Originally built as a rest home for teachers, it was later owned by the church and is now a holiday complex.

Holidaymakers like to pass the time in the pedestrianised zone on Norderney.

NATURAL GOLD MINE: THE WADDEN SEA

Every year the scene is the same: groups of people in waterproof boots and jackets congregate on the tidal flats to explore one of the most sensitive ecosystems in the world, the Wattenmeer or Wadden Sea between the mainland and the East Frisian Islands. Young visitors especially are fascinated by the animal gold mine that inhabits the rather boring-looking muddy sand of the Watt.

As this habitat is so unique, in 1986 the Lower Saxony Wadden Sea National Park was founded, its area covering an impressive 345,800 hectares or 854,470 acres. The parts that belong to the federal states of Schleswig-Holstein and Hamburg also have national park status and thus also enjoy special protection. In June 2009 the Lower Saxon flats, the Wadden Sea in the Netherlands and the section belonging to Schleswig-Holstein were made a UNESCO World Natural Heritage Site. Not only the ground itself is protected; the sandbanks, beaches, dunes, salt marshes and estuaries are also part of the conservation programme. There are mudflats all over the world but those off the East Frisian Coast are something special. Life here is very strongly influenced by the tide which goes in and out twice a day. At low tide the ground is dry, with only the rills full of water. People have lived with this constant change for many, many hundreds of years. Archaeologists have found traces of human settlement at Bensersiel going back over 2,000 years, for example.

Today's Wadden Sea is the second most productive ecosystem in the world after the tropical rainforest. It thus comes as no surprise to learn that up to 4,000 species of plant and animal thrive in the fertile habitat of the Watt. If you join a tour of the mudflats, you will soon notice little heaps of sand on the ground. This is waste excreted by a typical local inhabitant, the lugworm. It lives a few centimetres below the surface, with diatoms, snails, mussels and shrimp as its neighbours.

The snails that dwell here are a hot favourite with the common shelduck that spends the moulting season from July to September on the Wadden Sea. The population in Germany alone is estimated to be 180,000. Approximately 200,000 eider ducks also moult in the local mudflats. Scientists assume that about 1,000 pairs of eider duck breed here. The Watt is also a welcome place of rest for millions of migratory birds en route for Scandinavia, alongside between ten and twelve million waders, geese, ducks and gulls. And that isn't all. The salt marshes, sandy beaches and dunes are also a retreat and natural habitant for countless animals, including the pied avocet and the tern.

The wind is only prevented from eroding the dunes and blowing the sand on the beaches away by special plants only found on the tidal flats and the coast. These are sea lavender, sea holly and European beachgrass or marram grass, the latter chiefly responsible for reinforcing the dunes.

The natural habitat of the seal

And then there are the countless sandbanks. These are the natural habitat of the seal, the number of which has increased in the past few years – to the delight of the conservationists. You can observe them on special seal-watching trips from aboard a boat. However, the national park administration, based in Wilhelmshaven, the coastguards and particularly the people operating such tours are very careful not to disturb the animals. Those who come too close to the seals on private marine craft risk punishing fines – and could even lose their sailing licence.

Despite their great beauty the mudflats are not without danger. You should never go out on them without a guide. Unsuspecting wanderers can be quickly caught by the incoming tide. The weather can also change within minutes here and inexperienced walkers may easily lose their bearings. Many people have lost their lives in the Wadden Sea through sheer exhaustion ...

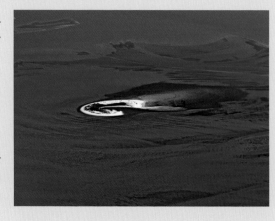

Left:
The atmospheric Wadden Sea near Borkum.

Above:
The habitat of the Wadden Sea is absolutely unique. Over centuries people on the coast have learned to live with the mudflats and to respect them.

Small photos, right, from top to bottom: Like the Rheiderland the Watt is especially beautiful at dawn and at dusk. The tidal flats provide many animals with a natural habitat and a vital source of food.

The seals of the Wadden Sae like to bask in the sun and tend to their young on the offshore sand dunes, such as here on the Tegeler Plate in the Weser Estuary.

The Wadden Sea may be beautiful but it is also dangerous. You should never go exploring without a trained guide.

The lugworm is possibly the most conspicuous inhabitant of the mudflats. The coils on the ground are its waste – which is entirely made up of sand, excreted as the worm munches its way through the Watt.

Even the smallest of the East Frisian Islands, Baltrum, caters for its religious community. The old island church was built in 1826. The minute chapel is often referred to as "God's dolls' house".

Baltrum is the smallest of the East Frisian Islands both in size and population. It's five kilometres or three miles long and a maximum of one kilometre or about half a mile wide, producing a surface area of 6.5 square kilometres or 2 ½ square miles.

None of the East Frisian Islands can do without their trains. They link the tiny harbours to the villages further inland, such as here on Langeoog.

In winter life on the islands is pretty sedate. The tourists have gone home and the locals can settle down to a quiet few months before the next holiday season starts.

Above:
The water tower from 1909 is very much Langeoog's local landmark. It was extensively restored in 2009 and also looks pretty in the snow.

Photos, left:
Most people are only familiar with the North Sea beaches in the summer. They are just as beautiful in winter, however, when snow and ice transform plants, grasses and footprints in the sand into works of art.

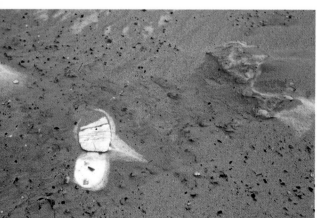

Below:
The island of Spiekeroog lies tucked in between Langeoog and Wangerooge. Like its counterparts, Spiekeroog is also devoid of cars, with only the fire brigade and rescue services motorised. There's no airport and there are even traffic restrictions for cyclists.

Top and centre right:
Spiekeroog has increasingly attracted the interest of various artists over the past few years. Rose gardens such as this one prove a great attraction for those armed with palette and easel.

Bottom right:
Low East Frisian cottages are typical of the islands – with this splendid rose gently clashing with the red brick.

129

Above:
This statue by Hannes Helmke entitled De Utkieker stands on top of Spiekeroog's highest sand dune. It was unveiled in June 2007.

Right:
The fine white sand along the North Sea Coast is paradise for children.

Left:
Marram grass or beach-grass is essential for the dunes on the North Sea Coast as it helps to keep the sand rooted to the ground, thus strengthening the structure.

Below:
An old beach hut on the North Sea Coast. These were once used to drive ladies down into the sea where they could enter the waves in their bathing attire in privacy.

Right:
The island of Wangerooge seen from the air. It is the easternmost of the seven inhabited East Frisian Islands and about eight kilometres or five miles in size.

Right:
Walking along the Wadden Sea at the eastern end of Wangerooge there is a good view of the Ostbake, an old beacon.

Far right:
Island architecture on Wangerooge. In the background you can see the old lighthouse.

Photos, right page:
Endless horizons and fantastic light: at sunrise and sunset the North Sea Coast of East Frisia is absolutely magical.

INDEX

....Text..Photo

134

Wangerooge

Spiekeroog

Langeoog

Norderney   Baltrum

e e

Minsener Oog

Mellum

Wangerooge

Spiekeroog

Langeoog   ★ Vogel-schutzgebiet

Baltrum

Norderney

erney

Weser

Harlesiel   Minsen

Friederikensiel   Schillighörn

Neuharlingersiel   Carolinensiel   *Wangerland*

Buddelschiff-museum   Neugarmssiel   Wanger-   Horumersiel

Dornumersiel   Bensersiel   Hohen-   land

Hilgen-riedersiel   Neßmersiel   Westerbur   Werdum   Altfunnix-siel   St. Joost

Hagermarsch   Nesse   Wasserschloss   ■ Esens   kirchen

Ostermarsch   *Oster-*   Bockwind-   Funnix   Tettens

Waloseum   *marsch*   Dornum   mühle   Stedesdorf   Hooksiel

rdeich   *Hager-marsch*   Museumsbahn   Holtgast

Linteler   Schloss   Arle   Ochtersum   Burhafe   Wadde-warden   Sengwarden

Marsch Nordeck   Schweindorf   Buttforde   Sillenstede   Niedersachsen-brücke

Ludgeri-kirche   Burg Berum   Großheide   Westerholt   Moorweg   Wiefels   *Jeverland*   Fedder-warden

Rathaus   Wasserschloss   Neuschoo   Blomberg   WITTMUND   JEVER   Schloss   Kopperhörner Windmühle

NORDEN   Lütetsburg   Eversmeer   SCHORTENS   WILHELMSHAVEN

Wester-marsch   Berumerfehn   *Ewiges*   Middels-Westerloog   Roffhausen   Kaiser-Wilhelm-Brücke

Charlotten-polder   Osteel   *Meer*   Ardorf   Sande   Oceanis

cht   Dietrichsfeld   Leerhafe   Cäcilien-groden   *Jadebusen*

ucht-older   Marienhafe   Upgant-   Victorbur   Tannen-hausen   *Pfalzdorfer*   Wasserschloss   Neustadt-gödens

Pfarrkirche   Schott   *Moor*   Kollrunge   Dangast

Grimersum   Wirdum   **Südbrookmer-**   Reepsholt

ahörn   Georgsheil   Moordorf   **land**   AURICH   Friedeburg

Pewsum   Upstalsboom   Neue Kanzlei   Marcards-moor

Wasserburg   Loppersum   Kirchloog   Marx

Hinte   Bedekaspel   Schirum   Holtrop   Zetel ■   Steinhausen

Groß   Suurhusen   *Großes*   Ludwigsdorf   Neuenburger   Bockhorn   VAREL

Midlum   *Meer*   Ihlow   Ost-   Wiesmoor   *Urwald*   Neuenburg

Hieve   Riepe   Ihlower-fehn   großefehn   Obenstrohe

EMDEN   Simons-wolde   Mitte-großefehn   **Großefehn**

Ostfriesisches   Timmel   Strackholt   Ockenhausen   Jade

arrelt   Landesmuseum   *Boekzeteler*   Neudorf   Bredehorn

Otthusen   *Meer*   Neukamper-fehn   *Lengener*   *Moor*

um   Borssum   Tergast   Firrel   Uplengen

Petkum   Oldersum   **Moormerland**   Schwerins-dorf   Remels   Halsbek

Ems-Sperrwerk   Warsings-fehn   Hesel

Ditzum   Neermoor   Veenhusen

Dollart   Hatzum   Holtland

Ditzumer-verlaat   Jemgum   Nüttermoor   WESTERSTEDE   Wiefelstede ■   ■ Rastede

Ems   Nortmoor

Bunder-hammrich   LEER   Filsum   Augustfehn

Bingum   Evenburg   *Jümme*   *Ammerland*

Bunderhee   Amdorf   Stick-   Vreschen-   *Zwischenahner*   *Meer*

Leda-sperrwerk   hausen   Bokel

Bunde   Weener   *Leda*   Potts-   hausen   Bad Zwischenahn

Holthusen   Ihrhove   **Rhauder-**   Collinghorst   **Ost-**   Barßel   *Hunte*

Mark   **Westover-**   **fehn**   **rhauder-**

Stapelmoor   Steenfelde   **ledingen**   Rhauder-moor   **fehn**   Strücklingen   Edewecht ■   OLDENBURG

Diele   Völlen   Völlenerfehn

Ems   Brual   PAPENBURG   *Saterland*   **DEUTSCHLAND**

Rhede   Aschendorf

OSTFRIESLAND   *Rheiderland*   *Overledingen*   *Harlingerland*   *Butjadingen*   *Jade*

10 km

This is one souvenir practically every visitor to East Frisia takes home with them.

Journey through East Frisia

Design
www.hoyerdesign.de

Map
Fischer Kartografie, Aichach

Translation
Ruth Chitty, Stromberg. www.rapid-com.de

All rights reserved

Printed in Germany
Repro: Artilitho snc, Lavis-Trento, Italien
        www.artilitho.com
Printed/Bound by Offizin Andersen Nexö, Leipzig
© 2011 Verlagshaus Würzburg GmbH & Co. KG
© Photos: Günter Franz
© Text: Ulf Buschmann

ISBN 978-3-8003-4136-8

Photo credits
All photos by Günter Franz with the exception of:
Page 16/17 and 41 (2 ill.): iStockphoto.com/Roland T. Frank; page 71 right above: Wikimedia Commons/ Fantast; page 91 second photo from top: Wikimedia Commons/Chris Hartmann; page 91 third photo from top: Wikimedia Commons/Evlaube; page 91 bottom: Wikimedia Commons/Christoph Grimlowski; page 113, left: iStockphoto.com/ideeone; page 113, right: iStockphoto.com/Stefan Franz; page 115 (3 ill.): iStockphoto.com/Jasmin Awad; page 124 and 132, bottom right: iStockphoto.com/Volker Rauch; page 132, bottom left: iStockphoto.com/Michael Schiffhorst

Details of our programme can be found at
www.verlagshaus.com